SUPER SNAKES

RATTLESNA

Murray "Oak" Tapeta

NorwoodHouse Press

Cataloging-in-Publication Data

Names: Tapeta, Murray.
Title: Rattlesnake / Murray Tapeta.
Description: Buffalo, NY : Norwood House Press, 2026. | Series: Super snakes | Includes glossary and index.
Identifiers: ISBN 9781978575165 (pbk.) | ISBN 9781978575172 (library bound) | ISBN 9781978575189 (ebook)
Subjects: LCSH: Rattlesnakes--Juvenile literature.
Classification: LCC QL666.O69 T374 2026 | DDC 597.96'38--dc23

Published in 2026 by
Norwood House Press
2544 Clinton Street
Buffalo, NY 14224

Designer: Rhea Magaro
Editor: Kim Thompson

Photo credits: Cover, p. 1 Donna Bollenbach/Shutterstock.com; p. 3 Jason Broome/Shutterstock.com; pp. 4, 5, 18 Chase D'animulls/Shutterstock.com; p. 6 onewildlifer/Shutterstock.com; p. 7 Matt Jeppson/Shutterstock.com; p. 8 Mark F Lotterhand/Shutterstock.com; p. 9 Nikolay Zaborskikh/Shutterstock.com; p. 10 MSMondadori/Shutterstock.com; p. 11 Pascal Halder/Shutterstock.com; p. 12 Danita Delimont/Shutterstock.com; p. 13 Clement Horvath/Shutterstock.com; p. 15 DMartin09/Shutterstock.com; p. 16 Maria Dryfhout/Shutterstock.com; p. 17 J.A. Dunbar/Shutterstock.com; p. 20 Mark_Kostich/Shutterstock.com; p. 21 DH Stanley/Shutterstock.com;

Printed in the United States of America

CPSIA compliance information: Batch #CSNHP26: For further information contact Norwood House Press at 1-800-237-9932.

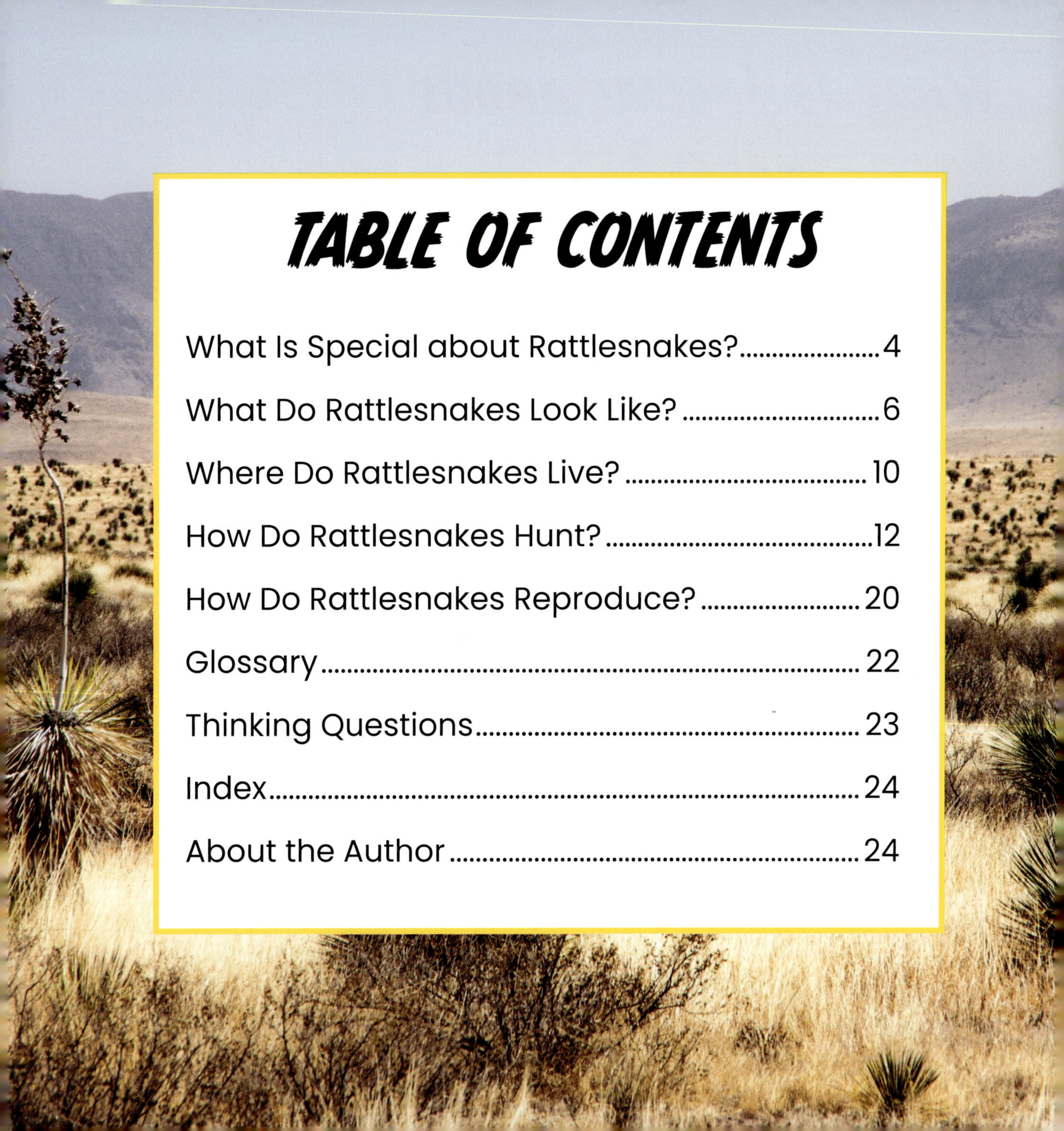

TABLE OF CONTENTS

What Is Special about Rattlesnakes?

A rattlesnake has a rattle at the tip of its tail. It is a stack of hollow, bony **segments**. A new segment gets added each time the snake **molts**.

When a rattlesnake feels threatened, it shakes its tail to give a warning. The bony parts bang together to make a rattling sound.

What Do Rattlesnakes Look Like?

There are at least 24 rattlesnake **species**. Rattlesnakes can be brown, black, gray, olive green, or yellow.

Most rattlesnakes have **markings**. The ridge-nosed rattlesnake is covered with brown and black patterns. They help the snake blend in with its surroundings.

Rattlesnakes come in many sizes. The eastern diamondback is the longest. It can grow eight feet (over two meters) long!

Rattlesnakes have triangle-shaped heads. Their **pupils** are narrow slits. This lets them see well even in low light.

Where Do Rattlesnakes Live?

Rattlesnakes live in North America, Central America, and South America. They like hot, sunny places. They are found in grasslands, forests, swamps, and deserts.

The sidewinder rattlesnake lives in deserts. To sneak up on prey, it buries its body in the sand.

How Do Rattlesnakes Hunt?

Rattlesnakes hunt small animals. They look for mice, rats, birds, lizards, frogs, and toads.

Rattlesnakes can wait weeks between meals. They may hide in the same spot for days, waiting for prey to show up. When the time comes, they **ambush** their victims.

A rattlesnake has a small hole, or pit, on each side of its face. The pits sense the body heat of prey animals. Snakes like this are known as pit vipers.

When a rattlesnake is ready to attack, it coils up. It launches one-third of its length toward the prey. It strikes with **fangs** that inject **venom**.

Small animals die soon after a rattlesnake bite. Most rattlesnake bites cannot kill humans.

Rattlesnakes swallow prey animals headfirst. Their stomachs **digest** the bones.

How Do Rattlesnakes Reproduce?

A female rattlesnake does not lay eggs. A male **fertilizes** eggs inside her body. Three months later, the female gives birth to live babies. Up to 25 babies can be born at one time.

Baby rattlesnakes stay close to their mother for about a week. The female protects her babies, but she does not feed them.

Glossary

ambush (AM-bush): to attack from a hiding place

digest (dye-JEST): to break down food so it can be used by the body

fangs (fangz): long, pointed teeth

fertilizes (FUR-tuh-lye-zis): provides the male parts that make a female's eggs able to grow into new life; joins male and female parts during mating

markings (MAHRK-ingz): colored lines, shapes, or patterns on the surface of something

molts (mohltz): sheds old skin, feathers, shells, or fur so that new body parts can grow

pupils (PYOO-puhlz): round, black centers of eyes that let light enter

segments (SEG-muhnts): parts or sections

species (SPEE-seez): groups of similar living things that can reproduce with each other

venom (VEN-uhm): a toxic substance that is produced by an animal to harm or kill prey and enemies

Thinking Questions

1. On what continents do rattlesnakes live?
2. What makes rattlesnakes different from other snakes?
3. What do rattlesnakes eat?
4. What do the pits on a rattlesnake's head do?
5. How do rattlesnakes eat their prey?

Index

About the Author

Murray "Oak" Tapeta was born in a cabin without plumbing in Montana. Growing up in the great outdoors, he became a lover of nature. He earned the nickname "Oak" after climbing to the top of an oak tree at the age of three. Oak loves to read and write. He has written many books about events in history and other subjects that fascinate him. He prefers spending time in the wilderness with his dog Birchy.